Ten Day Bible Study

Standing Firm on God's Word

Marie White

Zamiz Press
Publishing

Ten Day Bible Study

By Marie White

Categories: RELIGION / BIBLICAL STUDIES / BIBLE STUDY GUIDES

Copyright ©2015, Marie White

ISBN-13: 978-0-9992601-0-4

ISBN-10: 0-9992601-0-3

All rights reserved.

A special thanks to Jason White for his love, support and Godly counsel. Edited by P.M.B.

THE HOLY BIBLE, NEW INTERNATIONAL VERSION®, NIV® Copyright © 1973, 1978, 1984, 2011 by Biblica, Inc.® Used by permission. All rights reserved worldwide.

THE HOLY BIBLE, KING JAMES VERSION , public domain.

THE SCREWTAPE LETTERS, Copyright © 1942, C.S. Lewis Pte. Ltd.

Chapter heading logo designed by Sipa202- Pixabay.com

On Christ the solid rock I stand. All other ground is sinking sand.

- Edward Mote

From the hymn, *My Hope is Built on Nothing Less*, 1834.

MARIE WHITE

Ten Day Bible Study

Have you ever been at the beach and stood at the edge of the water? As the waves lap over your ankles, you can feel the sand beneath your feet slowly sift out from under you.

God uses this same illustration to tell us that if our spiritual foundation is not on His unchanging word, the Bible, then we might as well be on unstable sand.

I'd like to take you through ten days of detective work in your Bible so that you will have a firm foundation in God's word. It will equip you with answers to some of the most challenging questions about God, the Bible and Jesus.

As a missionary, traveler, adventurer and lover of people, nothing would make me happier than to share insights into God's word with you. You can connect with me at www.MarieWhiteAuthor.com where I am always available to answer questions.

This study is the follow-up to my YouTube series called *Bible Stories for Adults*, which is designed to take adult Christians through the entire Bible in two to five minute videos.

No matter what your level of Bible knowledge, this study will add new information to your spiritual life.

At the end of the study you will find a list of free resources, as well as recommended reading.

Let's take this journey together.

Contents

✝

Day 1:	Asking for Help	9
Day 2:	Arming for Battle	15
Day 3:	Mercy or Power	21
Day 4:	24 Hours	25
Day 5:	Prayer Secret	31
Day 6:	The Unknown God	35
Day 7:	Power in the Word	39
Day 8:	Standing Firm	45
Day 9:	Pray Like a Loser	49
Day 10:	At the Throne	53
Resources		59
Recommended Reading		60

Day One, Asking for Help

UNLESS OTHERWISE NOTED, ALL BIBLE VERSES ARE FROM THE NEW INTERNATIONAL VERSION (NIV) OF THE BIBLE.

Throughout the Bible God makes a number of promises. One promise that we can always cling to is that He is with us.

God reveals His love to His people through His interaction with them in both the Old and New Testaments.

The verses that we are about to read take place after the Jewish people are taken captive by King Nebuchadnezzar. This happens to the people as punishment for turning away from God (Daniel 1-2). They are brought to Babylon and the best and brightest are given high positions in the royal palace.

Let's read Daniel 3:1-30.

In your own words, paraphrase what Shadrach, Meshach and Abednego say in verses 16-18.

Now in James 1:6-7 it says, "But when you ask, you must believe and not doubt, because the one who doubts is like a wave of the sea, blown and tossed by the wind. That person should not expect to receive anything from the Lord."

Do you think that Shadrach, Meshach and Abednego were doubting God when they said, "even if he does not" in Daniel 3:18?

What makes you think that?

When Nebuchadnezzar looked into the furnace in Daniel 3:24-25, what did he see?

What Nebuchadnezzar saw is called a Christophany or Theophany, it is an appearance of Jesus before He was born as a human. The Chalcedonian Creed calls Jesus "fully God and fully man." John 1:1-3 says that Jesus existed before He was born to Mary, so His appearances in the Old Testament meant that at that time He was not fully man, only fully God, as a part of the trinity. While there were many Christophanies in the Old Testament, one of the more notable ones occurs in Genesis 18. Go ahead and read Genesis 18:1-33 and underline or highlight the words "Lord" and "I" in each verse.

What words in Genesis 18:17-19 let us know that it was not just an angel who appeared to Abraham?

What does John 1:1-18 say about Jesus existing before He was "born" as a human?

Shadrach, Meshach and Abednego gave their problem to God and trusted Him to fix it. They were also prepared to face the earthly penalty for their actions. They decided to follow God's commandment not to worship anything but Him (Genesis 20:1-6), even if God choose not to save them from the consequences. However, when God showed up He didn't just fix their problem, He also gained the worship of others.

What area of your life are you struggling in right now?

What is holding you back from giving that struggle to God and asking Him to fix it?

Let's ask God to fix it right now.

Lord God, You know the things that we each struggle with. Please give us clear direction on how to give those things to You and every time we try to take our struggles out of Your hands we ask You to make us let go. Teach us to trust in You. Give us power and hope. We ask these things in the most powerful name under heaven, the name of Jesus. Amen.

MARIE WHITE

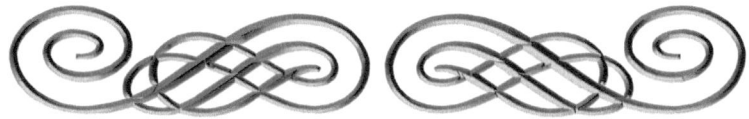

Day Two, Arming for Battle

Today we are going to begin by reading what Paul wrote to the church in the city of Ephesus in Ephesians 6:10-20. Who does this passage say that our battle is against?

Who does it say it is not against?

In verse 13, what does it say will come?

Does it say that it "might" come or that it "will" come?

Now look at 2 Corinthians 10:3-5.

One of the main points of that passage is that we are at war. Another point is that this war is nothing like the wars that we are used to. In verse 5 we read that we are supposed to "take captive every thought," what do you think that this means?

What does Matthew 6:34 give as possible reasons that God could have for wanting us to guard what we think about?

John 8:44 says that Satan "... was a murderer from the beginning, not holding to the truth, for there is no truth in him. When he lies, he speaks his native language, for he is a liar and the father of lies." If Satan is a liar and he can speak lies to us, would it be good to listen to those lies?

What thoughts have you had lately that you know are not from God and are harmful for you to dwell on?

What are some action steps that you can take to stop yourself from letting those thoughts get the best of you?

In Philippians 4:8 we read, "Finally, brothers and sisters, whatever is true, whatever is noble, whatever is right, whatever is pure, whatever is lovely, whatever is admirable—if anything is excellent or praiseworthy—think about such things."

When you feel like your thoughts are not pleasing to God, what are some things that you can think of instead that are:

True

Right

Pure

Praiseworthy

Lord God, we know that you want us to fix our eyes on You. Please help us to focus on You alone and not on the lies that we tell ourselves or that the enemy puts on us. When we do start to think about things that are not pleasing to You, we ask you to remind us again that we are Your children, that You love us and that You are have created us for a good purpose. Give us direction in all that we do. We pray this in Jesus' name. Amen.

MARIE WHITE

Day Three, Mercy or Power

Have you ever seen a plaque or poster with the words, "Be still and know that I am God?"

When I see beautiful, serene, pictures with those words I think of a soft voice from heaven whispering that to His children. Let's look at that verse today and see if that is what God really means.

Open your Bible to Psalm 46—but don't read it yet.

Imagine a medieval fortress sitting atop a lush, green hill in Scotland. The sky is dark grey and storm clouds race across the heavens. A cold wind rips across the water and waves are crashing against the rocks on the shore. Water is thrust upward every few minutes.

You notice red-orange flames leaping from a thousand battle shields burning in a pile and around them are remnants of war. Out of the corner of your eye you see bows and arrows cracked and broken across the landscape. The ground reeks of blood and desolation.

All of a sudden a voice booms from heaven and lightning streaks across the sky.

Now read Psalm 46.

Do you think that God was trying to soothe His people or remind them that He alone is all powerful?

Can you find any words that might indicate that God was not trying to soothe His people?

Now look at Job 38:1-11. Do you think that this was written in the same tone as Psalm 46?

What makes you think that?

When I read Psalm 46 I get the sense that God is not just full of mercy and tenderness but also full of power and might.

Would you feel more confident knowing that God is merciful or that He is powerful?

Psalm 103:8 says, "The Lord is compassionate and gracious, slow to anger, abounding in love."

We do not have to choose. God is big enough to be both compassionate and also mighty. He can be trusted with our hearts and yet He can annihilate our enemies.

In what area of your life do you need God's might today?

Lord God, when we forget just how powerful You are, please remind us. When we forget just how merciful You are, please remind us. And when we feel overwhelmed by this world, please remind us that we are just dust and that You forgive us for being weak. We ask this in Jesus' name. Amen.

Day Four, 24 Hours

In *The Screwtape Letters*, C.S. Lewis writes a letter from a senior demon to a junior demon. The senior demon is teaching the junior demon how to stop a man from becoming a Christian.

One of the tactics that he recommends is wasting the man's life.

The senior demon says that once a person learns to waste time;

"You no longer need a good book, which he really likes, to keep him from his prayers or his work or his sleep; a column of advertisements in yesterday's paper will do. You can make him waste his time not only in conversation he enjoys

with people whom he likes, but in conversations with those he cares nothing about on subjects that bore him. You can make him do nothing at all for long periods. You can keep him up late at night, not roistering, but staring at a dead fire in a cold room. All the healthy and outgoing activities which we want him to avoid can be inhibited and nothing given in return, so that at last he may say, as one of my own patients said on his arrival down here, "I now see that I spent most of my life in doing neither what I ought nor what I liked". The Christians describe (God) as one "without whom Nothing is strong". And Nothing is very strong: strong enough to steal away a man's best years not in sweet sins but in a dreary flickering of the mind."

Lewis' last words are chilling as he says that "nothing" is very powerful.

I am ashamed to think of how much time I have wasted watching TV or playing electronic games.

We are each given 24 hours. What we do with those 24 hours and the subsequent days, weeks, months and years is our choice. To use the time wisely think of ways that you can:

Serve others

Cultivate relationships

Impact lives

Get in shape

Inspire someone

Learn a new skill

I have heard stories of people whose only physical contact is when someone shakes their hand or hugs them at church.

You could have a profound effect on someone's life just by taking an interest in them, giving them a hug or sending a message to let them know that you are thinking of them.

Look around, who has God put in your life that could use a word of encouragement from you?

Turn to 2 Corinthians 1:3-4. What do those verses say that we are supposed to do?

What experiences have you been through that could be used to support or encourage another person?

Lord God, we bring before You all of the people in our lives. Please open our eyes to those You have put around us. Show us where You would like us to give the same love to others that You have given to us. Let us see people in the same way that You see them. Change our hearts to be more like Yours. In Jesus' name, amen.

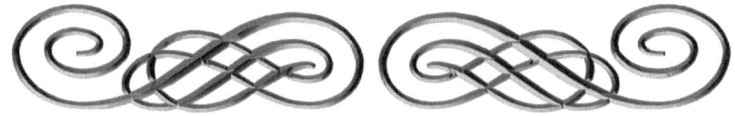

Day Five, Prayer Secret

We are going to read completely through two Psalms today. Are you ready? Do you think that you can read an entire chapter of the Bible in one day?

Here is Psalm 117,

> Praise the Lord,
>
> all you nations;
>
> extol him,
>
> all you peoples.
>
> For great is his love toward us,
>
> and the faithfulness of the Lord

endures forever.

Praise the Lord.

That was the entire Psalm. Did I scare you at first?

Now turn in your Bible to Psalm 138 and read it.

When is the last time that you gave someone a compliment without expecting something in return?

Today we will praise God and not ask anything from Him. Have you ever done that before?

It is not easy to praise God and not ask Him for anything, but it is worthwhile to attempt it. You may catch yourself turning your praise into a request, but try to fight that.

Read Psalm 104:31-34.

Now take a look at the first part of the Psalm that you just read. It says, "May the glory of the Lord endure forever; may the Lord rejoice in his works— he who looks at the earth, and it trembles, who touches the mountains, and they smoke."

Now we will take that Psalm and turn it into a prayer to God:

God, may Your glory endure forever. May You rejoice in Your works. You who look at the earth and make it tremble. You who touch the mountains and make them smoke.

It's your turn.

Read verses 33-34 and turn them into a prayer of praise to God by changing words such as "Lord", "God" and "him" to the word You.

How did that feel?

Do you think that including some sort of praise to God would be beneficial to your prayer life?

Do you think that God deserves it?

To end the day, look at Psalm 105:1-5.

Now pray it back to God as a praise to Him.

Lord God, thank you for being all that You are. Thank you for this opportunity to pray to You and to look with fresh eyes on just how magnificent You are. We will praise You with our hearts and with our lips because You are worthy of our praise. You are worthy of all praise. One day You will get the praise that You deserve. In the meantime we lift up our hands to You and offer You these few words and thoughts of just how marvelous You are. May Your name be praised forever. In Jesus' name, amen.

Day Six, The Unknown God

Has anyone ever asked you how a loving God could send someone go to hell?

Who?

How should you answer that question?

Look at Matthew 25:41.

In that verse who does Jesus say that hell was made for?

What does John 5:24 say that it takes for someone to get into heaven?

Based on those to verses could you conclude that God does not send people to hell, but that they choose to go there by not believing in Jesus?

Today we will look at common questions that God has already answered in His word.

Read Romans 1:18-23.

What does God say in verse 20 to people who would argue that they did not know about God?

Turn to Psalm 19:1-6. Other than another person telling us about God, what has He created to show Himself to us?

In the book, *Tortured for Christ**, Richard Wurmbrand tells the story of two communist artists that he meets. As sculptors, they realized that without a thumb they would be unable to create all of the things that they made. So, they decided to worship the maker of the thumb and when Richard told them who that maker was, they were elated.

God makes Himself known so that no one on earth has any excuse for not worshiping Him.

What things have you noticed around you that seem to point directly to God?

Roman's Road is a collection of Bible verses that explain God's plan to save us and how to become a Christian. If you do not already know these verses, it would be a great idea to write the references in the back of your Bible. That way you can find them for anyone who asks.

The verses are Romans 3:23, Romans 6:23, Romans 5:8 and Romans 10:9-10.

Lord God, please give us the words to say when people ask us about You. Give us the desire to read Your word and get to know You better. Thank you for giving us clear direction in Your word and through Your Holy Spirit. Please continue Your perfecting work in us. We ask this in Jesus' precious name. Amen.

*Get the book *Tortured For Christ* for free at www.persecution.com.

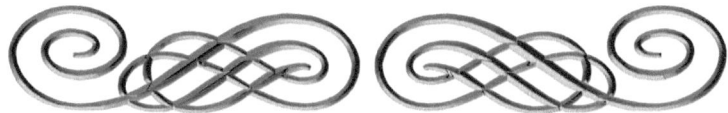

Day Seven, Power in the Word

How can you tell other people about God if you do not know Him yourself?

Daily Bible reading is not an optional exercise; it is the only way for a Christian to grow in faith and knowledge.

As a Christian it is important to read the entire Bible, every book, every paragraph, every line, so that you will have a complete understanding of who God is. If you only read a part of the Bible, then you will only know a part of God's story. His complete story was important enough for Him to write.

The Bible is God's love letter to His children. We should make the time to read it.

Have you read the entire Bible?

Why?

Statistically, Christians have the same divorce rate as non-Christians, this makes it seem like there is no difference between the lifestyle of the believer and the non-believer. But is this true? Are all of the people who call themselves Christians really Christians?

What makes a person a Christian?

Where does it say that in the Bible?

If you can't answer that question, then Acts 16:29-34 will help.

What does Acts say about being a Christian?

To learn more about living as a Christian, look up these verses and write them in the back of your Bible; 2 Timothy 2:15, Hebrews 10:25, and 2 Timothy 3:1-15.

Have you ever been asked a question about Jesus that you could not answer?

How did that make you feel?

Have your actions as a Christian ever been questioned?

When we mess up it is tempting for us to use the excuse that no one is perfect. But it's funny that it's an excuse that only seems applicable when we talk about obeying God.

How many people could use that excuse when their boss asks why they aren't at work? How many people could say that when they haven't paid their taxes? How many people could claim imperfection as the reason that their children are not taken care of?

Zig Ziglar said that each morning he reads his Bible and the newspaper, that way he knows what both sides are up to. One woman made the decision to stop painting her nails so that she would have time to read her Bible. Some people will not check email or texts in the morning until they have read their Bible.

What things in your life could be removed or rearranged to allow you to have time to read God's love letter to you?

If you knew the Bible inside and out, what would that do for your confidence in speaking to others about Jesus?

How would reading the Bible improve your life in other ways?

Matthew 13:22-23 says, "The seed falling among the thorns refers to someone who hears the word, but the worries of this life and the deceitfulness of wealth choke the word, making it unfruitful. But the seed falling on good soil refers to someone who hears the word and understands it. This is the one who produces a crop, yielding a hundred, sixty or thirty times what was sown."

Do not let the hustle and bustle of life choke out your Bible reading time. It only takes five minutes a day.

Pray before you start reading your Bible and ask God to make His word come alive for you.

He will answer that prayer. I guarantee it.

Lord God, please keep our eyes on You and You alone. Stop us from being distracted by this world. We know that all power, peace and knowledge come from You. Invade our hearts and minds, take over any areas that we have not yet given to You and transform us so that we are more like You and less like ourselves. Thank you for hearing us when we call out to You. We pray this in Jesus' name. Amen.

Day Eight, Standing Firm

Are you a super-Christian?

When we started going to church we bought paperback NIV Study Bibles. Once we had been going for a few years our Bibles began to come apart so we purchased Bibles with leather-like covers and gold edges. A friend noticed our new Bibles at church one Sunday and we jokingly said that now we were super-Christians.

God doesn't say that we have to be super-Christians, but He does warn us that not everyone who calls themselves a Christian is one.

Go ahead and read Matthew 7:21-27.

What does God say that a person must do to build his house on the rock in verse 24?

What does that mean in your life?

We can get a better understanding of what God is talking about by going to Matthew 7:13-20.

What does fruit mean?

If the majority of people in America call themselves Christians, how can we use verses 13-20 to test that?

In the talk *True and False Conversion*, Ray Comfort says that there are certain fruits that show up in a Christian's life when they are a believer.

Read Colossians 1:10-12.

In that passage do you see the fruits of: good works - growing in understanding of Jesus – patience - endurance - giving thanks to God?

In which areas in your life would you like to bear more fruit?

Satan is our accuser. Revelation 12:10 calls him, "the accuser of our brothers and sisters, who accuses them before our God day and night."

When we look at the areas of our lives that are not bearing good fruit, it would be easy to get caught up in Satan's accusations that we are not good enough to serve God. As Pastor Greg Laurie says, we *aren't* good enough. Agree with the enemy and deflate his balloon. God's love for us and our acceptance of Jesus' sacrifice to cover our sins are the only two reasons that we are good enough to get into heaven.

Lord God, we thank You that You are bigger than our problems and bigger than our fears. Whatever we face may seem daunting to us, but to You it is smaller than a grain of sand. Please teach us to keep our eyes focused on You and to compare our struggles to Your power. You said that if we have faith we can tell a mountain to fall into the sea and it will be done. We ask You to move mightily and guide us through life. We ask all of this in Jesus' holy name. Amen.

Day Nine, Pray Like a Loser

Today I would like you to read 1 Chronicles 4:9-10. If you are able, read these verses in the HCSB or NKJV.

What four requests did Jabez make?

What was God's answer to Jabez's request?

Your "territory" is the area of influence that you have. What is your specific territory?

According to this passage, is it wrong to ask God to bless you?

Someone else asks for a blessing in Genesis 27:38. Who asks for this blessing?

Esau asked his father for this after he had traded his inheritance to this brother for some soup. Selling your rights to the larger portion of the family inheritance for a cup-o-lentils isn't a very smart move. But what it also shows is that Esau did not value his position as the eldest brother. He didn't value his birthright. Esau then loses his blessing, as his brother disguises himself and gets his father to bless him in Esau's place. That is when Genesis 27:38 happens.

Hebrews 12:16-17 elaborates on this verse, saying that Esau was a profane man and that he was not sorry for his actions.

Who asks for a blessing in Exodus 12:31-32?

Do Esau's request and Pharaoh's request for blessing come from the same motive of the heart as the request that Jabez makes?

What makes you think that?

Lord God, please guide us in everything that we think and do so that we are always seeking Your will and doing it. Make the things that are important to You, be important to us. You say to pray about everything and we want to do that. If there is some area of our lives that we are supposed to be asking You for guidance about, please bring it to our minds so that we can ask You about it. We ask You to bless us abundantly and to enlarge our influence so that we can reach others for You. We ask this in the name of Your son, Jesus. Amen.

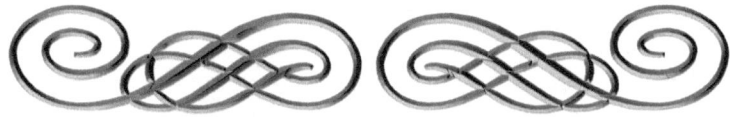

Day Ten, At the Throne

This is the last day of our Bible study together. If you have enjoyed it then maybe you'd enjoy doing another one. Take a look at your local Christian store and check out their selection of Bible studies.

For our last day of Bible study let us give our praises to God.

Turn to Psalm 119:49-64.

Now read that section and turn each line around as a thank you to God such as:

Lord God, I thank you for remembering Your word and Your servant, for You have given me hope. Thank you that my comfort in my sufferings is that Your promise preserves my life.

Continue until you have prayed all of Psalm 119:49-64 as a prayer of thanksgiving.

We are never happier than when we take our eyes off of our problems and look to God. He makes every problem seem small.

Are you in a good place right now or are you in the middle of a spiritual or physical battle?

If you could give one problem to God and have it resolved forever, what would it be?

Write out a prayer thanking God in advance for fixing that problem. If you need inspiration, look again at Psalm 119:49-64.

(prayer continued)

Each of us has our own picture of heaven. While none of them will be accurate, there might be some accuracy in our feelings or emotions toward heaven. Part of my picture of heaven (after worship, crowns, singing, passing from judgment, etc.) is a moment when I can sit at God's feet, at his throne, lay my head on his knees, and as He strokes my hair He says, "The pain is all over and new life has begun."

What do you imagine your perfect "heaven" moment to be?

Please read Revelation chapter 4, chapter 21 and chapter 22.

Whatever grandness we could imagine, whatever descriptions He gives us in Revelation, our minds cannot conceive of the real majesty of heaven.

The Bible gives us descriptions of streets of gold, walls of jewels, crowns and riches—but they don't make sense to us. What God has made is too great for our human minds to comprehend.

What part of Revelation's description of heaven surprises you?

Romans 14:10-12 and Philippians 2:10 say that every knee will bow and every tongue will confess that Jesus is Lord. As Christians, we choose to do it now, willingly, but the time is coming when everyone will do it…willing or not.

Heaven is real. We are going there.

Is there is anything that is hindering your relationship with God?

If so, now is the moment to fix it.

Lord God, if there is anything in our hearts that is keeping us from following You wholeheartedly, please remove it. We know that we are not perfect enough to get into heaven, but that You sent Jesus to die for us so that His blood would wash over our sins and make us able to appear before You. You said that if we confess our sins to You and ask for Your forgiveness then You would give it. We ask that today. Any sins that need forgiveness, we set them before You and ask You to make them go away. Then we ask that You make us Your children. Pure and clean before You. So that we can spend forever with the most wonderful, loving and perfect father. You. We ask for this in the most powerful name under heaven, the name of Jesus. Amen.

Resources

Free Movies:

The Gospel of John
www.ebiblemovies.org/watch/gospel-of-john/online-free/

Unlocking the Mystery of Life
https://youtu.be/tzj8iXiVDT8

The Fingerprint of God
https://youtu.be/7Uo4Oond1e8

Bible Reading Plans:

New Testament- http://tinyurl.com/j3kxsuy

Old Testament- www.biblestudytools.com/bible-reading-plan/

Online Sermons:

James MacDonald
www.jamesmacdonald.com/tv/

Greg Laurie www.harvest.org

Recommended Reading

The Prayer of Jabez by Bruce Wilkinson

Left Behind by Tim Lahaye and Jerry B. Jenkins

This Present Darkness by Frank Peretti

Faith on Trial by Pamela Binnings Ewen

The Hiding Place by Corrie Ten Boom and Elizabeth Sherrill

The Purpose Driven Life by Rick Warren

NIV Study Bible by Zondervan

The Jesus I Never Knew by Philp Yancey

The Case for Christ by Lee Strobel

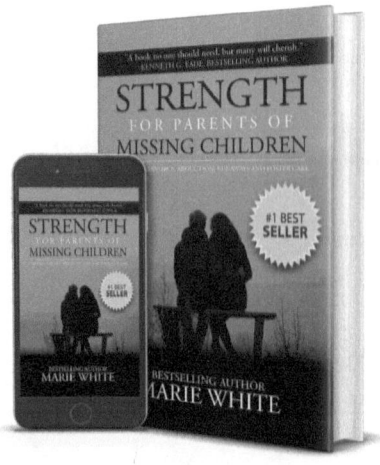

Marie White is the bestselling author of many books, including *Strength for Parents of Missing Children*. She is also the host of the popular YouTube series, **Bible Stories for Adults**, which reaches people in every part of the world.

She is a missionary, traveler and lover of people. She endeavors to love people by sharing God's word..

To learn more about the Bible, watch her YouTube video series, **Bible Stories for Adults**.

For a FREE BOOK or to contact the author please visit www.MarieWhiteAuthor.com.

Instagram @MarieWhiteAuthorOfficial
Tweet to @MarieWritesBook

Are you looking for a way to share Christ with your friends and family in the LGBT community?

God's Love for LGBTQI by Marie White.

Available in paperback and Kindle editions.

MARIE WHITE

www.ingramcontent.com/pod-product-compliance
Lightning Source LLC
Chambersburg PA
CBHW022229010526
44113CB00033B/783